Music Minus One
VOCALS

10 FAVORITES WITH SOUND-ALIKE DEMO & BACKING TRACKS ONLINE

ED SHEERAN

PLAYBACK+
Speed • Pitch • Balance • Loop

To access audio visit:
www.halleonard.com/mylibrary

Enter Code
3077-1224-0822-8048

Cover Photo by Mark Venema/Getty Images

ISBN: 978-1-5400-2654-5

Visit Hal Leonard Online at
www.halleonard.com

Contact Us:
Hal Leonard
7777 West Bluemound Road
Milwaukee, WI 53213
Email: info@halleonard.com

In Europe contact:
Hal Leonard Europe Limited
Distribution Centre, Newmarket Road
Bury St Edmunds, Suffolk, IP33 3YB
Email: info@halleonardeurope.com

In Australia contact:
Hal Leonard Australia Pty. Ltd.
4 Lentara Court
Cheltenham, Victoria, 3192 Australia
Email: info@halleonard.com.au

CONTENTS

THE A TEAM

Words and Music by
ED SHEERAN

say she's in the Class A team. Stuck in her day-

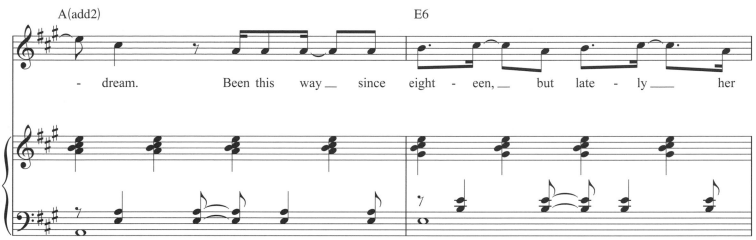

-dream. Been this way since eight-een, but late-ly her

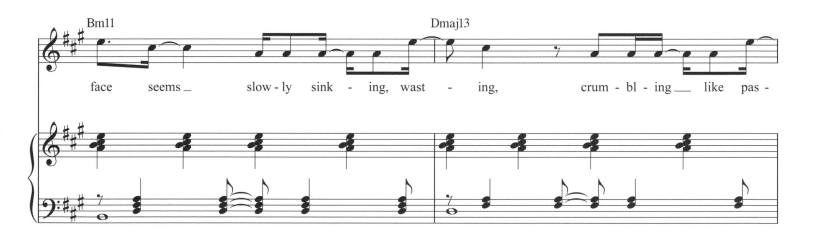

face seems slow-ly sink-ing, wast-ing, crum-bl-ing like pas-

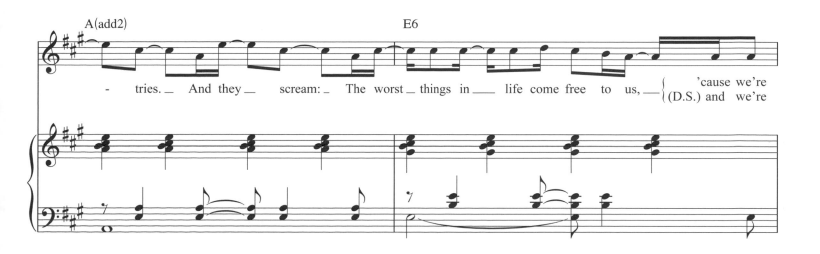

-tries. And they scream: The worst things in life come free to us, { 'cause we're (D.S.) and we're

ALL OF THE STARS
from the Motion Picture Soundtrack THE FAULT IN OUR STARS

Words and Music by ED SHEERAN
and JOHNNY McDAID

Moderately slow

It's just an-oth-er night and I'm star-ing at the moon.
I can hear your heart on the ra-di-o beat;

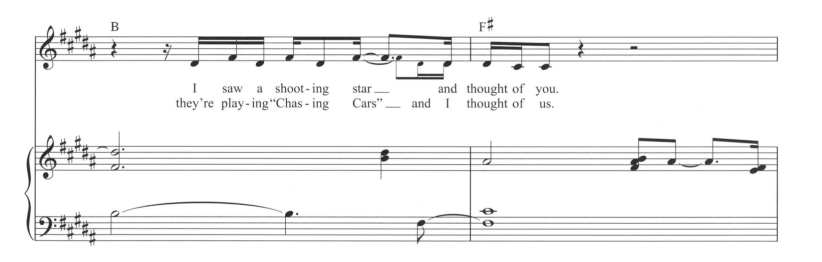

I saw a shoot-ing star and thought of you.
they're play-ing "Chas-ing Cars" and I thought of us.

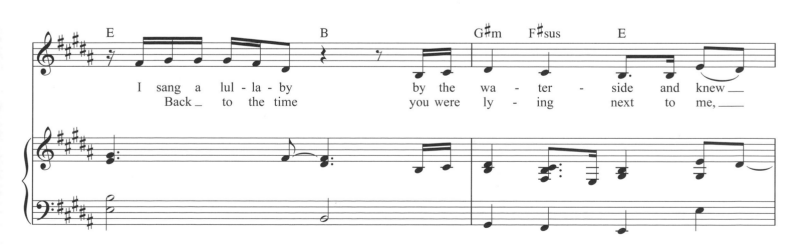

I sang a lul-la-by by the wa-ter-side and knew
Back to the time you were ly-ing next to me,

CASTLE ON THE HILL

Words and Music by ED SHEERAN
and BENJAMIN LEVIN

And I've not seen ___ the roar - ing fields ___ in so ___ long. I ___
Me and my friends ___ have not ___ thrown up ___ in so ___ long: oh,

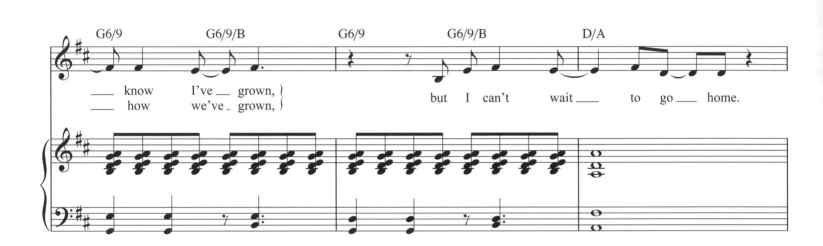

___ know I've ___ grown, }
___ how we've ___ grown, }
but I can't wait ___ to go ___ home.

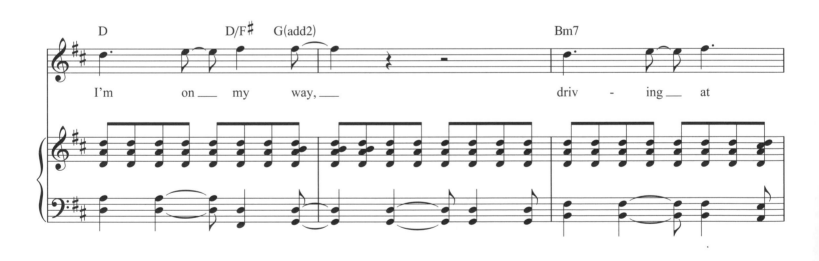

I'm on ___ my way, ___ driv - ing ___ at

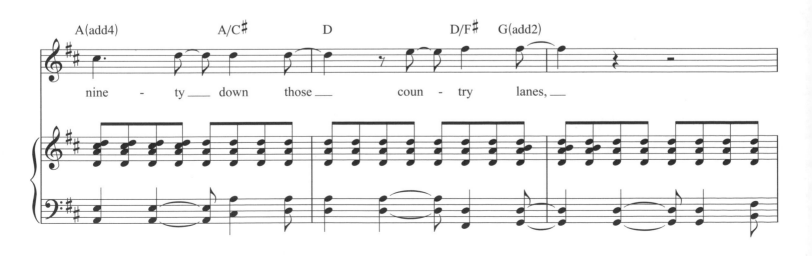

nine - ty ___ down those ___ coun - try lanes, ___

GALWAY GIRL

Words and Music by ED SHEERAN,
FOY VANCE, JOHN McDAID,
AMY WADGE, EAMON MURRAY,
NIAMH DUNNE, LIAM BRADLEY,
DAMIAN McKEE and SEAN GRAHAM

Moderately

She played the fid-dle in an I-rish band, but she fell in love with an Eng-lish man. Kissed

—— her on the neck and then I took her by the hand, said, "Ba — by, I just —— wan-na dance." I met her on

Graf-ton Street, right out-side of the bar. —— She shared a ci-ga-rette with me while her broth-er played the gui-tar. She asked me,

Gal - way _____ girl."

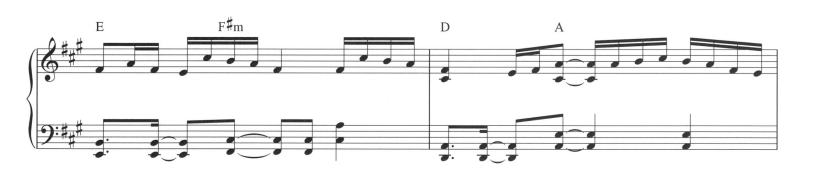

GIVE ME LOVE

Words and Music by ED SHEERAN,
CHRIS LEONARD and JAKE GOSLING

Moderately, in 2

Give me love, like her.

LEGO HOUSE

Words and Music by ED SHEERAN,
CHRIS LEONARD and JAKE GOSLING

50

PHOTOGRAPH

Words and Music by ED SHEERAN,
JOHNNY McDAID, MARTIN PETER HARRINGTON
and TOM LEONARD

Loving can hurt.

Loving can hurt____
Loving can mend____

some-times.
your soul.

But it's the on - ly thing that I____
And is the on - ly thing that I____

PERFECT

Words and Music by
ED SHEERAN

Moderately, in 4

I found a love ____ for ____ me.

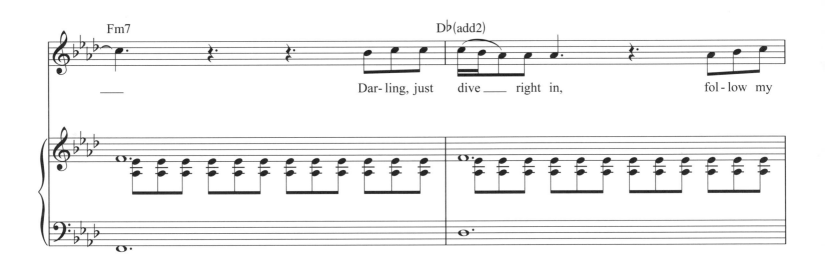

Dar-ling, just dive ____ right in, fol-low my

lead. Well, I found a girl, ____ beau-ti-

CODA

you look per - fect to-night."

Ba - by,_____ I'm _____ danc - ing in the

dark with you be-tween my arms. Bare - foot on the

SHAPE OF YOU

Words and Music by ED SHEERAN,
KEVIN BRIGGS, KANDI BURRUSS,
TAMEKA COTTLE, STEVE MAC
and JOHNNY McDAID

To Coda

THINKING OUT LOUD

Words and Music by ED SHEERAN
and AMY WADGE

(La, la,   la,   la, la, la,   la, la, la,   la, la, la.)

D.S. al Coda

So hon- ey, now, _

CODA

where   we   are.   Ba - by,   we   found   love   right

where   we   are. _____   And   we   found   love   right   where   we   are. _

ORIGINAL KEYS FOR SINGERS

Titles in the Original Keys for Singers series are designed for vocalists looking for authentic transcriptions from their favorite artists. The books transcribe famous vocal performances exactly as recorded and provide piano accompaniment parts so that you can perform or pratice exactly as Ella or Patsy or Josh!

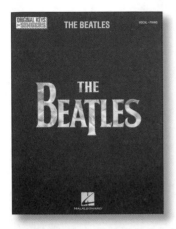  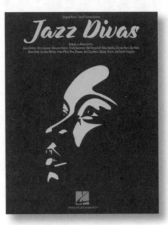 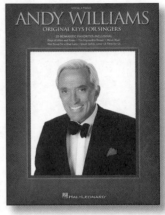

ACROSS THE UNIVERSE
00307010..$19.95

ADELE
00155395..$19.99

LOUIS ARMSTRONG
00307029..$19.99

THE BEATLES
00307400..$19.99

BROADWAY HITS (FEMALE SINGERS)
00119085..$19.99

BROADWAY HITS (MALE SINGERS)
00119084..$19.99

PATSY CLINE
00740072..$22.99

ELLA FITZGERALD
00740252..$17.99

JOSH GROBAN
00306969..$19.99

BILLIE HOLIDAY
Transcribed from Historic Recordings
00740140..$17.99

ETTA JAMES: GREATEST HITS
00130427..$19.99

JAZZ DIVAS
00114959..$19.99

LADIES OF CHRISTMAS
00312192..$19.99

NANCY LAMOTT
00306995..$19.99

MEN OF CHRISTMAS
00312241..$19.99

THE BETTE MIDLER SONGBOOK
00307067..$19.99

THE BEST OF LIZA MINNELLI
00306928..$19.99

ONCE
00102569..$16.99

ELVIS PRESLEY
00138200..$19.99

SHOWSTOPPERS FOR FEMALE SINGERS
00119640..$19.99

BEST OF NINA SIMONE
00121576..$19.99

FRANK SINATRA – MORE OF HIS BEST
00307081..$19.99

TAYLOR SWIFT
00142702..$16.99

STEVE TYRELL – BACK TO BACHARACH
00307024..$16.99

SARAH VAUGHAN
00306558..$19.99

VOCAL POP
00312656..$19.99

ANDY WILLIAMS – CHRISTMAS COLLECTION
00307158..$17.99

ANDY WILLIAMS
00307160..$17.99

www.halleonard.com

Prices, contents, and availability subject to change without notice.